D1042628

Detoxify the
with artichokes, asparagus, and other cleansing foods
Natural Way

HEALTH ALL YEAR ROUND

Treating your body to an "inner spring cleaning" contributes to vitality and well-being. Delicious, detoxifying foods stimulate the metabolism, purify the blood, rid the body of excess fluid, and put the liver, gallbladder, and kidneys into tiptop working order. The traditional time for a "detox" is in the spring–the Christian practice of fasting for Lent is a typical example. In the weeks leading up to Easter, there is an abundance of foods ideal for the purpose of detoxifying, such as the first tiny artichokes and baby asparagus. However, many detoxifying foods are available all year, so you can really perform a spring cleaning in any season.

A SLUGGISH SYSTEM

Nature normally takes care of the "ins" and "outs" of the food we eat. If the "outs" part of the process is no longer functioning as well as it might, unwanted by-products and waste substances can accumulate in the body. These impurities are deposited in the blood vessels, joints, tissues, organs, and muscles, and can show in one's appearance.

In the long run, serious illnesses can result. The first indications that impurities are building up in the body are constant fatigue, lack of concentration, listlessness, chronic headache, and susceptibility to infections. Skin breakouts, frequent digestive upsets, and muscle and joint pain can also signal the need for a detox. These are warning signals given by your body–take them seriously. To combat these ailments, treat your body to a general overhaul. Carefully planned menus, conscious enjoyment of the foods themselves, sufficient exercise in the open air, adequate periods of relaxation, and a little skin and body pampering will do you good. You will emerge feeling as if you are new born.

Organs responsible for Detoxification

Liver: The liver can be described as the body's own chemical factory–a great variety of chemical transformation processes happen here. The liver's key role is enabling the body to use the food eaten by breaking down certain substances and forming others. As bodies age, they absorb more and more harmful substances, such as alcohol, caffeine, cigarette smoke, car exhaust fumes, and other toxins. The task of putting things right falls on the liver, and if it is not in good shape, we will feel the ill effects. The liver also manufactures bile, which is particularly important for the digestion of fats.

Kidneys: Consider the kidneys the blood's filter. The blood flows through the kidneys many times a day to sift out any nutritionally useful substances, which are returned to the circulation, and any harmful substances that are present in excess. The latter are excreted in urine made by the kidneys. Overtaxing the body with impurities, such as medications and alcohol, or frequent urinary infections, can, in the long run, damage the kidneys and/or cause them to cease functioning.

Intestines: A healthy intestinal flora acts on the food in the gut, taking out any nutritionally useful substances that have not yet been digested, and leaving the useless ones to be excreted. The greatest enemies of intestinal flora are antibiotics and food with too little roughage. Both hinder the smooth functioning of the digestive processes, damage the intestinal flora, and enable metabolic breakdown products to accumulate.

Lungs: The role of the lungs in detoxifying the body mainly involves expelling carbon dioxide, filtering out toxic substances from the air we breathe, and removing toxins present in the blood. Heavy smokers face an increased risk of damaging the lungs and affecting their detoxifying abilities.

Skin: Healthy skin protects the body against unwanted invaders. Sweating also rids the body of harmful substances through the skin's pores.

Fitness

Detoxify yourself for a healthy feeling

Inside and Out

DAILY SELF-HELP GEMS

* Drink plenty of fluids. This is important to flush out the kidneys and carry away metabolic breakdown products.
* Keep active. Good exercise includes breathing in plenty of oxygen–the more you do this, the better your metabolism will be.
* Take the time to eat properly, and be sure to chew slowly. The digestion of carbohydrates begins in the mouth.
* Eat a low-fat diet. Fat is the last nutrient to be digested from the food, and it is a slow process. The liver will be taken up with its share of the task for a long time, leaving little time for its detoxification role.
* Avoid alcohol, tobacco, and medications as much as possible. Metabolizing these substances makes great demands on your body's detoxification organs.
* Treat commercially prepared meals as a last resort. They often contain many additives, such as flavorings and flavor enhancers, spelling hard work for the liver. They may also contain hidden fats, which will jeopardize your eating plan.

CHOOSE YOUR FOODS WISELY

* Eat plenty of carbohydrates, especially fiber-rich foods. The roughage present in these items promotes the activity of the intestines, making it more difficult for unwanted substances to accumulate.
* Select foods that provide a good amount of vitamins and minerals. These enable all the processes of the body to take place efficiently. Sufficient vitamins and minerals ensure thorough removal of waste products– the key to a detoxification plan. Some vitamins are essential components of digestive juices.
* Eat raw fruit and vegetables as often as you can. Cooking destroys important nutrients in these foods. Raw foods also contain quantities of certain digestive enzymes, which are beneficial to the body.
* Consume many base-forming foods, which will protect the body from excess acid. Raw fruit, vegetables, and salad greens are good examples. A diet too rich in acid-forming substances, such as meats, sweets, alcohol, coffee, and tea, imposes a great deal of work on the liver and kidneys.

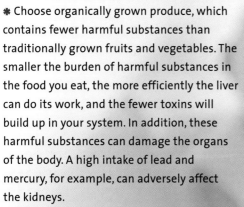

✻ Choose organically grown produce, which contains fewer harmful substances than traditionally grown fruits and vegetables. The smaller the burden of harmful substances in the food you eat, the more efficiently the liver can do its work, and the fewer toxins will build up in your system. In addition, these harmful substances can damage the organs of the body. A high intake of lead and mercury, for example, can adversely affect the kidneys.

✻ Choose fresh vegetables and fruits whenever possible. If not possible, choose frozen. Vegetables for freezing are freshly picked, so they offer the best chance of still containing their valuable nutrients.

✻ For those who wish to use them, there are several preparations to assist in simple, speedy detoxification and ridding the body of excess fluid; health food stores and pharmacies stock these. For example, artichokes and asparagus can be found as juices, or in tablet form. Other juices available are from bean, nettle, watercress, pumpkin, dandelion, parsley, black radish, and other plants with health-giving properties. Delicious, healthy cocktails can be mixed using some of these, together with fresh fruit and vegetable juices. Of course, this should be in addition to eating fresh foods.

Cleansing

Foods to remember in a detox plan

Foods

FRUIT AND VEGETABLES

ARTICHOKES: Contain *cynarin*, which stimulates the liver and gallbladder, promotes the flow of blood through them, cleanses them, and also promotes the digestion of fats. Artichokes help rid the body of excess fluid (diuretic) and lower the cholesterol level

ASPARAGUS: Contains aspartic acid, which is a strong diuretic; stimulates the kidneys; and has a positive effect on the body's metabolism. Also contains potassium, which helps rid the body of excess fluid

BELGIAN ENDIVE: Contains the bitter constituent *intybin*, which contributes to the proper function of the liver, gall-bladder, stomach, and intestines; stimulates digestion and metabolism; cleanses the system; helps rid the body of excess fluid; promotes blood formation

FENNEL: Contains volatile oils that stimulate liver and kidney activity; promotes digestion

KOHLRABI: Stimulates the flow of bile, and is beneficial to the kidneys; promotes blood formation

LEEKS: Promote digestion; cleanse the intestine; contain mustard oils, which stimulate the liver, gallbladder, and kidneys; help rid the body of excess fluid

PINEAPPLE: Contains the enzyme *bromelin*, which promotes metabolism and helps rid the body of excess fluid

POTATOES: Help rid the body of excess fluid

RADISHES: Contain volatile oils, which stimulate digestion and the formation of bile; unblock biliary flow; help rid the body of excess fluid

HERBS AND SPICES

BURNET: Helps rid the body of excess fluid (diuretic)

DILL: Stimulates urine flow

GARDEN CRESS: Purifies the blood; helps rid the body of excess fluid; stimulates metabolism

GINGER: Stimulates circulation; promotes appetite and digestion

HORSERADISH: Helps rid the body of excess fluid; stimulates stomach, gallbladder, kidneys, and intestines

JUNIPER: Purifies the blood; helps rid the body of excess fluid

LOVAGE: Stimulates the flow of bile and secretion of stomach digestive juices; promotes kidney activity

NASTURTIUM: Stimulates the formation of red blood cells; purifies the blood; encourages the transport of oxygen around the body

NETTLE: Purifies the blood; increases urine flow. Contains an excess of bases, so it's good for de-acidification

PURSLANE: Purifies the blood and helps in blood formation; helps rid the body of excess fluid

ARUGULA: Regenerates the mucous lining of the gut; helps rid the body of excess fluid

TARRAGON: Helps rid the body of excess fluid; stimulates metabolism; cleanses the kidneys and gallbladder

TURMERIC: Fortifies the liver and gallbladder; purifies the blood; increases production of bile

SUBSTANCE	EFFECT	IMPORTANT SOURCES
Bitter constituents	strengthen the glands that produce digestive juices, stimulate the gallbladder; promote the digestion of fats	broccoli, artichokes
Calcium	combats the heavy metals lead and cadmium, preventing their storage in the body	milk, nuts, broccoli, green cabbage
Chloride	regulates the acid-base balance; detoxifies	almost all foods
Fiber	stimulates the activity of the intestines, shortening the time that the food remains in the gut; absorbs metabolic and other waste products in the stomach and intestines, so that they can be eliminated	grains, leafy green vegetables, peas, carrots, potatoes, apples, pears, berries
Glutathione	speeds up detoxification processes in the body	leafy green vegetables, radishes, root vegetables
Hot constituents	stimulate digestion	spices such as ginger, chiles, pepper, paprika
Iron	promotes blood formation; important for transport of oxygen	peas, beans, spinach, nuts, cabbage, grapes, red meat
Mustard oils	have a purifying and antiseptic effect; increase activity of stomach and intestines; strengthen liver, gallbladder, kidneys, and bladder	cabbage, radishes, root vegetables, onions, leeks
Potassium	rids the body of excess fluid and stimulates kidney activity; strengthens blood vessels and kidneys	potatoes, cabbage, brown rice, fruit, grains
Secondary plant substances	protect against free radicals, which are involved in the buildup of impurities in the body; help the cleansing process; can be diuretic	fruit and vegetables
Selenium	binds heavy metals and enables their elimination from the body; stimulates the liver; important for deactivating free radicals	almost all types of fruit and vegetables, red cabbage, grains, nuts, meat
Volatile oils	stimulate the metabolism, helping to remove harmful substances; stimulate appetite and digestion; cleanse mucous membranes; strengthen the stomach, liver, gallbladder, and intestines	many plants, especially herbs and spices; also fennel, carrots, celery
Zinc	aids in combating stress; decreases the burden on the liver	fish, meat, cheese, grains

Power
Detoxify with a feast of vitamins
Week

FEELING BETTER THROUGH EATING, NOT FASTING

Would you like to lavish a little more attention on yourself and pay more attention to your health? Do you wish you could banish that weary feeling–not just in the spring– and perk up your metabolism? Treat your body to a week of detoxifying meals, and you're bound to feel better–without feeling deprived. Prepare and eat the recipes given for this one-week eating plan, and in no time you will start feeling and looking healthier. Of course, you can prepare any of the recipes anytime to give your health and well-being a kick.

THE ONE-WEEK DETOX PLAN

Following are suggestions for seven days' worth of meals. You can follow the plan as given, or mix and match the recipes if you wish. The best start to the day is a breakfast of whole-grain bread or whole-grain granola with sliced fruit, and low-fat yogurt or cottage cheese. If you get hungry, snack on raw fruit and vegetables. Use the tables on pages 6 and 7 to select the varieties that cleanse the body. For best results, it is important to drink as much liquid as possible during your detoxifying Power Week; however, avoid beverages with large amounts of sugar and caffeine. Spring water, of course, is ideal.

AT WORK ALL DAY?

If you're too busy to prepare two meals a day, you can still reap the benefits of a detox plan. Prepare one of the recipes for the evening meal. To the office, bring some fresh fruit, vegetables, and yogurt for the midday meal. Use the tables on pages 6 and 7 to help you choose detoxifying produce.

THE WEEK'S MEALS

Monday

* Low-fat granola with fresh fruit, or whole-grain black bread; buttermilk
* Harlequin Vegetable Salad; whole wheat baguette
* Asparagus and Shrimp Risotto; fresh pineapple

Tuesday

* Whole-grain black bread; acidopholous milk
* Salad of Endive and Cress * Quick Potato Curry
* Brown Rice and Celery Root Pancakes; fresh fruit

Wednesday

* Low-fat granola with fresh fruit, or whole-grain black bread; buttermilk
* Watercress Soup * Asparagus and Herb Omelet
* Linguine with Artichoke Sauce; fresh pineapple

Thursday

* Whole-grain black bread; acidopholous milk
* Cornmeal Patties with Radish Salad; Fresh fruit
* Arugula and Apple Salad; sautéed boneless chicken breast

Friday

* Low-fat granola with fresh fruit, or whole-grain black bread; buttermilk
* Fruit and Asparagus Salad; whole-wheat baguette
* Salmon with Sorrel Sauce; new potatoes; fresh pineapple

Saturday

* Whole-grain black bread; acidopholous milk
* Vegetable and Yogurt Bake
* Julienned Zucchini with Red Pepper Sauce; whole-grain black bread;
Potato Cream Soup with Arugula

Sunday

* Fresh fruit salad; whole-wheat rolls; lean cold meats; one egg
* Chervil in Aspic with Mustard Sauce * Stuffed Artichokes
* Asparagus Salad with Prosciutto; baguette; fresh pineapple

Asparagus
Salad with
and crunchy pine nuts
Prosciutto

Serves 2: 1 lb white or green asparagus • Salt to taste • 1/2 tsp sugar • 1 tsp butter •

2 tbs cider vinegar • White pepper to taste • 3 tbs vegetable oil • 4 thin slices prosciutto

• 2 tbs pine nuts • Fresh basil leaves

Wash and trim the asparagus, and peel the lower third of the stalks. Bring a small amount of water to a boil in a saucepan with a little salt, the sugar, and butter. Place the asparagus in a steamer insert and lower it into the saucepan. Cover tightly and steam for 5-8 minutes, until the asparagus is tender-crisp.

In a bowl, mix together the cider vinegar, salt, and pepper; then, thoroughly beat in the oil with a whisk. Drain the asparagus well and cut into chunks. Toss the asparagus in the dressing. Arrange on plates with the prosciutto. Toast the pine nuts in a dry nonstick skillet until golden. Scatter the nuts over the asparagus, adding a few fresh basil leaves, for garnish.

PER PORTION: 358 calories • 17 g protein • 32 g fat • 7 g carbohydrates

Asparagus Salad
fresh herbs add a refined touch
with Watercress

Serves 2:
1 lb asparagus
Salt to taste
1/2 tsp sugar
1 tsp butter
1/2 bunch watercress
1-2 tbs walnuts
1-2 tbs chopped mixed
fresh herbs
1 tbs cider vinegar
White pepper to taste
1 tbs walnut oil
2 tbs vegetable oil

Wash and trim the asparagus, and peel the lower third of the stalks. Bring a small amount of water to a boil in a saucepan with a little salt, the sugar, and butter. Place the asparagus in a steamer insert and lower it into the pan. Cover tightly and steam for 5-8 minutes, until the asparagus is tender-crisp. Drain well and cut into chunks.

Wash the watercress well and shake dry. Sort it, removing any coarse stems. Roughly chop the walnuts.

To make the dressing, mix the herbs with the vinegar and season with salt and pepper. Thoroughly beat the two oils into the mixture with a whisk. Season to taste.

Toss the asparagus and watercress in the dressing. Arrange on plates and sprinkle with the walnuts.

Watercress

This peppery salad green (or herb) is full of good and healthy things. Just 5 oz supplies the entire daily requirement of vitamin C. It also contains iron, important in blood formation, and calcium. Watercress purifies the blood and encourages the flow of urine, making it an ideal ingredient in a detox plan.

PER PORTION:

251 calories

6 g protein

22 g fat

7 g carbohydrates

power

Dandelion Greens Salad
a stylish springtime salad
with Goat Cheese

Preheat the oven to 425°F. Peel and chop the onion and garlic and whisk them together with the vinegar, salt, and pepper. Thoroughly beat in the oil using a whisk.

Wash and sort the dandelion greens. Shake thoroughly dry and tear into bite-sized pieces. Toss the leaves in the dressing and arrange on plates. Wash the cherry tomatoes, halve or quarter them, and add to the salad.

Cut the goat cheese into four rounds and lay on top of the bread slices. Place in an ovenproof dish and bake on the middle oven shelf until the cheese is hot, but not yet melted. Place the bread on the plates with the salad and serve immediately.

Serves 2:
1 small onion
1 small clove garlic
1-2 tbs wine vinegar
Salt to taste
White pepper to taste
3 tbs safflower oil
4 oz baby dandelion greens
2 oz small cherry tomatoes
1 small round goat cheese (2 oz)
4 baguette slices

Dandelion greens

Dandelion greens contain substances that stimulate the appetite and the digestion. Kidney activity is enhanced by dandelion greens, which therefore have a diuretic effect. A bitter constituent, *choline*, acts on liver function, and encourages the flow of bile. Dandelion is popular as a medicinal plant for treating gallbladder, liver, and kidney problems.

power

PER PORTION:

339 calories

11 g protein

19 g fat

9 g carbohydrates

Fennel and
with sautéed pork tenderloin
Grapefruit Salad

Peel the grapefruit with a very sharp knife, removing all of the bitter white pith. Cut down the sides of each membrane to release the fruit segments, collecting the juice in a bowl. Wash the fennel, trim it, and slice the bulb very finely. Chop the green fennel fronds and set aside.

Serves 2:
1 pink grapefruit
1 bulb fennel
1 shallot
Salt to taste
Black pepper to taste
1 tbs cider vinegar
3 tbs canola oil
1/2 thin pork tenderloin
3 juniper berries
1 small handful arugula

Peel and finely chop the shallot. Whisk it together with the fennel fronds, salt, pepper, and vinegar in a bowl. Use a whisk to beat in 2 tbs of the oil, followed by the reserved grapefruit juice. Toss the fennel bulb and grapefruit segments in the dressing.

Rinse the pork with cold water and pat dry. Crush the juniper berries using a mortar and pestle, or chop with a large knife. Rub the pork with the crushed juniper berries, salt, and pepper. Heat the remaining 1 tbs oil in a large skillet over medium-high heat. Brown the meat on all sides, then reduce the heat to medium, and continue to cook for about 5 minutes, until done.

Wash the arugula, shake dry, and sort. Arrange on plates with the fennel and grapefruit salad. Cut the pork into thin slices and arrange on plates with the salad.

PER PORTION: 323 calories • 14 g protein • 23 g fat • 18 g carbohydrates

Purslane Salad
with slightly sweet apple dressing
with Green Beans

Serves 2:
3 oz green beans
Salt to taste
1 sprig fresh summer savory
or thyme
2 oz small white mushrooms
5 radishes
2-3 oz purslane
1 shallot
1 small clove garlic
Black pepper to taste
1 tbs cider vinegar
2 tsp unfiltered apple juice
(purchased or homemade)
2 tbs canola oil

Rinse and trim the beans, and halve if necessary. Bring a small quantity of salted water to a boil in a saucepan with the savory or thyme. Place the beans in a steamer insert, lower them into the saucepan, cover tightly, and steam for 10-15 minutes, until tender-crisp.

Meanwhile, rinse the mushrooms, or clean with a damp cloth. Slice them finely. Rinse and trim the radishes and cut into thin slices. Wash the purslane, shake dry, sort, and trim.

To make the dressing, peel and chop the shallot and the garlic. Stir them together with the salt, pepper, cider vinegar, and apple juice. Whisk in the oil thoroughly.

Drain the beans well and toss them in the dressing with the mushrooms, radishes, and purslane. Adjust the seasonings.

Purslane

This vegetable has green, fleshy leaves, which are rich in potassium and iron. Purslane helps flush out the system, and assists in blood formation. It also contains healthy omega-3 fatty acids.

PER PORTION:

123 calories

3 g protein

8 g fat

10 g carbohydrates

power

Raw Parsnip and Carrot Salad

a winter health boost

Toast the walnuts in a dry nonstick skillet until golden brown. Remove from the heat. Coarsely chop about 3 tbs of the walnuts and set aside. Grind the remaining walnuts finely, and mix them with the cream, milk, oil, and vinegar, stirring until smooth. Season with coriander, salt, and pepper. Select a small amount of the green parsnip tops, wash, shake dry, and chop finely. Stir the parsnip tops into the dressing.

Rinse and trim the parsnips and carrot. Slice them thinly or grate them. Arrange the vegetables on plates, drizzle with the dressing, garnish with the reserved chopped walnuts, and serve immediately.

Serves 2:

2 oz walnuts
1/4 cup heavy cream
1/4 cup milk
2 tsp safflower oil
1 tbs cider vinegar
Ground coriander to taste
Salt to taste
Black pepper to taste
5 oz parsnips (with tops)
1 small carrot

Parsnips

Parsnips are a good source of vitamins in the cold season of the year, when many other vegetables are unavailable. Just 7 oz of parsnips contain the daily requirement of vitamin C. In addition, parsnips stimulate the appetite and promote the flow of urine.

PER PORTION:

235 calories

5 g protein

17 g fat

18 g carbohydrates

power

Asparagus and
with crisp croutons
Avocado Salad

Cut away the crusts from the bread. Cut the bread into small dice. Heat the butter in a small saucepan until foaming. Fry the diced bread in the butter until golden brown on all sides. Cool.

Wash and trim the green onion and slice finely. Stir together with the apple juice, vinegar, salt, and pepper. Thoroughly beat in the two oils with a whisk. Rinse and trim the asparagus, and carefully peel the lower third of the stalks. Cut it diagonally into thin slices, and toss the slices in the dressing.

Wash the tomatoes, cut into wedges, and remove the tough portion next to the stalk. Peel the avocado, cut it in half, and remove the pit. Cut each half crosswise into slices. Sprinkle the slices with lemon juice.

Arrange the tomato wedges, avocado slices, and asparagus mixture on plates, sprinkling the tomatoes and avocado with some of the dressing. Scatter the croutons over the top.

Wash the lemon thyme and shake dry. Strip the leaves from the stalks and scatter over the salad. Serve immediately.

Serves 2:

1 slice whole-grain bread
1 tsp butter
1 small green onion
2 tsp unfiltered apple juice
(purchased or homemade)
1 tbs cider vinegar
Salt to taste
White pepper to taste
1 tbs canola oil
1 tbs walnut oil
9 oz white or green asparagus
2 small, firm tomatoes
1 small avocado
1-2 tbs fresh lemon juice
1-2 sprigs fresh lemon thyme

power

PER PORTION: 243 calories • 4 g protein • 18 g fat • 17 g carbohydrates

Light
with yogurt dressing and pecans
Waldorf Salad

Serves 2: 1 super-fresh egg yolk • 2 tsp fresh lemon juice • 2-3 tbs canola oil • 1/4 cup plain yogurt • Salt to taste • Black pepper to taste • 2 stalks celery with leaves • 1 oz pecans • 1-2 tart apples

Stir together the egg yolk and lemon juice, then slowly whisk in the oil drop by drop. Stir in the yogurt. Season with salt and pepper. Rinse and trim the celery. Reserve the leaves and slice the stalks. Chop the nuts coarsely. Wash the apples, and cut them into 1/2-3/4-inch dice, removing the cores. Toss all the ingredients in the dressing, check the seasonings, and serve garnished with the reserved celery leaves.

PER PORTION: 325 calories • 5 g protein • 26 g fat • 20 g carbohydrates

Julienned Zucchini
a crunchy, vitamin-packed treat
with Red Pepper Sauce

Serves 2: 1 red bell pepper • Salt to taste • Black pepper to taste • Tabasco sauce to taste • 1 shallot • 1 small clove garlic • 1 tbs cider vinegar • 2 tbs olive oil • 4 oz zucchini

Rinse and trim the red pepper. Cut into fourths, and dice one piece finely. Puree the rest and push the puree through a sieve. Season the pepper puree with salt, pepper, and a few drops of Tabasco, and divide among serving plates. Peel and chop the shallot and the garlic, stir into the vinegar, season with salt and pepper, and beat in the oil with a whisk. Wash and trim the zucchini and cut into fine strips. Toss the strips in the dressing, then arrange on top of the red pepper sauce. Garnish with the diced red pepper.

PER PORTION: 101 calories • 2 g protein • 8 g fat • 5 g carbohydrates

Arugula Salad with

a cleansing salad with a taste of Italy

Two Cheeses

Toast the pine nuts in a dry nonstick skillet until golden brown. Set aside.

Trim and sort the arugula, wash it, and shake dry. Tear it into smaller

pieces if necessary. Peel the carrot and grate it

coarsely. Cut the fontina cheese into strips. Grate the

Parmesan cheese.

To make the dressing, peel the shallots and dice very

finely. Whisk together with the balsamic vinegar,

salt, and pepper. Then, beat in the oil thoroughly

with a whisk. Adjust the seasonings.

Toss the arugula, grated carrot, and fontina cheese in

the dressing. Sprinkle the salad with the pine nuts

and grated Parmesan.

Serves 2:

2 tbs pine nuts

3 oz arugula

1 small carrot

2 oz fontina cheese

1 oz piece Parmesan cheese

2 small shallots

2 tbs balsamic vinegar

Salt to taste

Black pepper to taste

1/4 cup olive oil

Arugula

Also called rocket or rucola, this well-loved
salad green (or herb) is a relative of cabbage
and mustard greens. Like them, it contains
volatile oils and organic acids, whose effect on
the appetite is stimulating . Arugula is also
rich in vitamin C. It rids the body of excess
fluid and should certainly be featured on the
menu in any detox plan.

PER PORTION:

346 calories

13 g protein

32 g fat

6 g carbohydrates

Harlequin
with herbs and pumpkin seeds
Vegetable Salad

Cut the red pepper in half, trim away the stem and inner ribs, and remove the seeds. Wash it. Peel the kohlrabi, and trim and wash the radishes, reserving a little of the green tops of both. Wash or peel the cucumber.

Serves 2:

1 small red bell pepper
1 small kohlrabi
1/2 bunch radishes
4 oz cucumber
1 small onion
1 small clove garlic
2 tbs pumpkin seeds
4 sprigs fresh Italian parsley
Handful of fresh chervil
4 sprigs fresh dill
1 sprig fresh tarragon
2 tbs cider vinegar
Salt to taste
Black pepper to taste
2 tbs safflower oil
1 tbs pumpkin seed oil

Cut the red pepper, kohlrabi, and cucumber into approximately 1/2-inch dice. Slice the radishes thinly. Mix the vegetables together.

Peel and finely chop the onion and garlic. Put them into a salad bowl. Chop the pumpkin seeds and add to the mixture in the salad bowl. Wash the herbs, along with the kohlrabi and radish tops, shake them dry, and chop. Add the herb mixture to the salad bowl.

Put the vinegar in a small bowl, and season generously with salt and pepper. Beat in the two oils with a whisk. Adjust the seasonings, then pour into the bowl with the vegetables and toss well. Let the salad stand for 30 minutes to blend the flavors.

PER PORTION: 219 calories • 7 g protein • 18 g fat • 9 g carbohydrates

Fruit and

with strawberries and melon

Asparagus Salad

Wash the asparagus, trim it, and carefully peel the lower third of the stalks. Bring a small amount of water to a boil in a saucepan with the

Serves 2:
10 oz green asparagus
1 tsp butter
Salt to taste
Sugar to taste
1/4 ripe cantaloupe
3 oz fresh strawberries
1 tbs cider vinegar
1 tsp honey
White pepper to taste
3 tbs canola oil

butter and a little salt and sugar. Place the asparagus in a steamer insert and lower it into the pan. Cover securely and steam for 5-8 minutes, until the asparagus is tender-crisp.

Meanwhile, remove the seeds and fibers from the melon. Use a melon baller to scoop out little balls of the flesh. Wash and drain the strawberries, trim, and halve or quarter them.

In a salad bowl, whisk together the cider vinegar, honey, and a little salt and pepper. Thoroughly beat in the oil with a whisk. Drain the asparagus thoroughly and cut it into pieces about 1$\frac{1}{4}$ inches long. Toss the asparagus in the dressing, together with the melon and strawberries. Serve immediately.

PER PORTION: 167 calories • 3 g protein • 13 g fat • 9 g carbohydrates

Sauerkraut Salad
cleansing and rich in vitamins
with Cress

In a salad bowl, thoroughly whisk together the cider vinegar, apple juice, and oil. Season with salt, pepper, and curry powder. With a knife, cut the sauerkraut into small pieces. Toss it in the dressing. Carefully peel the pineapple, removing the brown "eyes." Cut out the tough middle core and dice the flesh. Cut the ham into dice or strips.

Rinse the cress under cold water and shake dry. Trim the cress and put it in the bowl with the pineapple and ham, and toss well.

Season the salad generously, and arrange it on serving plates garnished by the nasturtium leaves and flowers.

Serves 2:

2 tsp cider vinegar

1 tbs unfiltered apple juice (purchased or homemade)

2 tbs canola oil

Salt to taste

Black pepper to taste

1/4 tsp curry powder

5 oz sauerkraut (drained)

1/4 fresh pineapple

2 oz boiled ham

1/2 bunch peppercress

Small handful nasturtium leaves and flowers

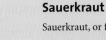

Sauerkraut

Sauerkraut, or fermented cabbage, contains lactic acid and fiber to stimulate digestion. Lactic acid also has a cleansing effect. Fresh, raw sauerkraut is the most beneficial to the intestinal flora and digestion, and to health in general. It contains up to 60 percent more vitamins than canned sauerkraut. Look for it in a high-quality delicatessen or specialty foods store.

PER PORTION:

203 calories

6 g protein

12 g fat

19 g carbohydrates

Arugula and

light, refreshing, and crisp

Apple Salad

Toast the pine nuts in a dry nonstick skillet until light golden brown. Set aside.

Wash the apple thoroughly, quarter, and core it. Dice the apple and sprinkle it

immediately with the lemon juice.

Trim and sort the arugula, wash it, and shake it

thoroughly dry. Tear into smaller pieces if necessary.

To make the dressing, whisk together the apple juice,

red wine vinegar, salt, and pepper in a bowl. Then,

thoroughly beat in the two oils with a whisk. Adjust

the seasonings. Toss the arugula and diced apple in

the dressing. Arrange the salad on plates and scatter

the reserved pine nuts over the top. Grate the

Parmesan over the salad before serving.

Serves 2:

2 tbs pine nuts

1 small red-skinned apple

1 tbs fresh lemon juice

3 oz arugula

1 tbs unfiltered apple juice
(purchased or homemade)

2 tbs red wine vinegar

Salt to taste

Black pepper to taste

2 tbs olive oil

1 tbs pine kernel oil

1 oz Parmesan cheese

Alternatives to pine kernel oil

If you can't find pine kernel oil, or for a variation on the
salad, other oils and nuts can be used instead. For
example, use walnut oil and walnuts, hazelnut oil and
hazelnuts, or almond oil and almonds. For a less intense
flavor, dilute the nut oil with a neutral one.

PER PORTION:

245 calories

5 g protein

20 g fat

15 g carbohydrate

power

Fresh Herb Salad

with velvety Parmesan sauce

with Dry-Cured Beef

Serves 2:
3 oz mixed fresh herbs
2 oz dry-cured beef (such as
Swiss Bundnerfleisch)
1 egg
2 tbs canola oil
3 tbs dry white wine
2 tbs cider vinegar
2 oz Parmesan cheese, grated
3 tbs plain yogurt
Salt to taste
Black pepper to taste

Wash the herbs thoroughly and shake dry. Pick them over, and remove the tough stalks. Cut the dry-cured beef into strips and mix with the herbs.

Whisk the egg in a bowl with the oil, wine, and vinegar. Place the bowl over a saucepan of hot water and cook over medium heat, whisking constantly, until a light, creamy sauce is formed.

Remove the bowl from the pan of hot water, and stir the Parmesan into the sauce until melted. Cool the sauce a little, stir in the yogurt, and season with salt and pepper. Arrange the herb mixture on plates, drizzle the sauce over it, and serve immediately.

Herbs

Wild or cultivated, all herbs are full of health-giving properties. Fragrant and low in calories, they stimulate the appetite and digestion, and help cleanse the system. Try dandelion greens, watercress, sorrel, basil, Italian parsley, and chervil. Or, use dandelion greens or arugula alone.

PER PORTION:

265 calories

20 g protein

18 g fat

1 g carbohydrates

power

Radish and
raw food with a touch of elegance
Kohlrabi Carpaccio

Serves 2: 1/2 bunch radishes • 2 small kohlrabi • 1 tbs balsamic vinegar • 1 tbs unfiltered apple juice (purchased or homemade) • 1/4 tsp mustard • Salt to taste • Black pepper to taste • 2 tbs olive oil • 2 tsp pumpkin seed oil • 1 tbs pumpkin seeds

Wash and trim the radishes and kohlrabi. Peel the kohlrabi. Slice both vegetables thinly. Mix the vinegar, apple juice, mustard, salt, and pepper. Beat in the two oils. Arrange overlapping slices of kohlrabi in a circle on each plate. Arrange the radish slices inside the ring, circle in overlapping slices. Drizzle the dressing over the top and garnish with the pumpkin seeds.

PER PORTION: 154 calories • 3 g protein • 12 g fat • 11 g carbohydrates

Salad of Endive
a vitamin boost for chilly days
and Cress

Serves 2: 2 small oranges • 5 tbs plain yogurt • Salt to taste • White pepper to taste • Ground coriander to taste • 2 tbs grapeseed oil • 1-2 tbs ketchup • 8 oz Belgian endive • 1/2 bunch peppercress

Peel and segment the oranges, collecting the juice in a bowl. Mix the juice with the yogurt, salt, pepper, coriander, grapeseed oil, and ketchup. Wash and trim the endive, and cut into pieces. Rinse the cress under cold water, shake dry, and trim. Arrange the orange and endive on serving plates, drizzle with the dressing and scatter the cress over the top.

PER PORTION: 146 calories • 4 g protein • 6 g fat • 18 g carbohydrates

Watercress

tempting and cleansing

Soup

Wash the watercress and remove any very tough stems. Set aside a few leaves for garnish. Peel and finely dice the onion. Melt 1/2 tbs of the butter in a saucepan over medium heat and sauté the onion in it until transparent. Add the watercress and sauté briefly. Add the vegetable stock and simmer for a few minutes over low heat.

Puree the soup in a blender and return it to the saucepan. Stir in the cream and bring the soup back to the boiling point.

Place the egg yolk in a cup and stir in a little of the hot soup until smooth. Pour the mixture back into the pan with the soup, and stir well; do not allow the soup to boil at this stage. Season the soup with salt and a few drops of lemon juice.

Melt the remaining 1/2 tbs butter in a skillet. Cut the bread into dice and sauté it in the butter until browned on all sides and crisp. Scatter the croutons over the soup before serving, and garnish with the reserved watercress leaves.

Serves 2:
1/2-1 bunch watercress
1 small onion
1 tbs butter
1 cup vegetable stock
1/2 cup heavy cream
1 egg yolk
Salt to taste
Lemon juice to taste
1-2 slices whole-grain bread

PER PORTION: 364 calories • 6 g protein • 23 g fat • 28 g carbohydrates

Potato Cream Soup

with crunchy almonds

with Arugula

Serves 2:
10 oz potatoes
1 small onion
2 tsp butter
2 cups vegetable stock
2 tbs sliced almonds
1 small handful arugula
Salt to taste
White pepper to taste
5 tbs heavy cream

Peel, wash, and dice the potatoes. Peel and dice the onion. Melt the butter in a saucepan over medium heat and sauté the onion in it until translucent. Add the diced potato and the stock, cover, and simmer for 10-15 minutes over low heat. Meanwhile, toast the almonds in a dry nonstick skillet until light golden brown. Remove from the heat. Wash the arugula and shake it dry. Remove any tough stems and cut the rest into strips. Puree the potato soup in a blender. Return it to the saucepan and bring it back to the boiling point. Season with salt and pepper. Add the strips of arugula to the soup. Stir the cream into the soup. Garnish with the almonds before serving.

Soup with a plus

The potassium-rich potatoes and the aspartic acid-rich arugula, with its diuretic properties, both play a part in cleansing. The extra liquid from the soup is a bonus: it flushes out the kidneys.

PER PORTION:

299 calories

5 g protein

19g fat

26g carbohydrates

power

Creamy Lentil
with smoky bacon
Soup

Put the lentils and vegetable stock in a saucepan and bring to a boil.

Reduce the heat to low and simmer, covered, for about 40 minutes.

Cut the bacon into thin strips. Wash and trim the green onions, and cut them diagonally into small rings. Take a few lentils from the soup and set aside. Puree the remaining soup in a blender, and return it to the saucepan. Stir in the cream and reserved lentils and bring it back to the boiling point. Season with salt, pepper, and mustard; the soup should be boldly flavored.

Fry the bacon in a nonstick skillet until crisp. Add the green onions and toss them briefly in the bacon fat, without frying. Season with pepper.

Pour the soup into bowls, sprinkle the bacon and green onions on top, and serve immediately.

Serves 2:

1/3 cup lentils

2 cups vegetable stock

1 oz bacon

1/2 bunch green onions

5 tbs heavy cream

Salt to taste

Black pepper to taste

1/2 tsp mild mustard

Lentils and mustard

Lentils are rich in fiber, which stimulates and protects the intestines, and prevents impurities from collecting. Mustard contains the glycoside *sinigrin* and the enzyme *myrosin*. Moisture causes them to react with each other, releasing volatile mustard oil, which has a cleansing, antiseptic effect on the body.

PER PORTION:

355 calories

14 g protein

21 g fat

25 g carbohydrates

power

Salmon and
light and luxurious
Asparagus Soup

Wash and trim the asparagus. Peel it carefully, reserving the trimmings and peelings. Cut off the tips and set aside, covered. Cut up the asparagus stalks and

Serves 2:
10 oz white or green asparagus
2 cups water
Salt to taste
Sugar to taste
2 tbs butter
4 oz fresh peas in the pod
(about 2 oz when shelled)
4 oz salmon fillet
1 tbs fresh lemon juice
1 tbs flour
1/4 cup crème fraîche

place in a saucepan with 1/2 cup of the water, a pinch each of salt and sugar, and 1/2 tsp of the butter. Bring to a boil, cover, and cook for 15 minutes. Puree the cooked asparagus pieces with their cooking liquid.

Meanwhile, place the asparagus trimmings and peelings into another saucepan. Add the remaining 1 cup water, a pinch each of salt and sugar, and 1/2 tsp of the butter. Cover and simmer for 15 minutes. Strain and reserve the cooking liquid, discarding the solids.

Meanwhile, shell the peas. Wash the salmon and cut it into dice. Sprinkle it with the lemon juice.

Melt the remaining butter in a saucepan over medium-low heat. Stir in the flour and cook until the mixture turns golden brown. Pour in the strained asparagus cooking liquid and stir well; add the asparagus puree and crème fraîche.

Place the asparagus tips, peas, and salmon in the soup, and cook through for 2-3 minutes. Season the soup and serve immediately.

PER PORTION: 291 calories • 15 g protein • 21 g fat • 10 g carbohydrates

Chilled Cucumber
refreshment for hot summer days
Soup

Serves 2: 9 oz cucumber • 5 oz plain yogurt • 5 tbs crème fraîche • 1/2 cup buttermilk • 1 clove garlic • Salt to taste • Black pepper to taste • 1 tomato • 2 sprigs fresh dill

Peel the cucumber and grate it coarsely. Place it in a bowl and stir in the yogurt, crème fraîche, and buttermilk. Peel the garlic, mince it finely, and stir it into the soup. Season with salt and pepper. Cover and chill for 2 hours. Wash the tomato and dill. Dice the tomato finely. Select the delicate fronds of the dill and pull them away from the coarser stalks. Scatter the dill fronds and tomato onto the soup and serve.

PER PORTION: 240 calories • 6 g protein• 20 g fat • 9 g carbohydrates

Sauerkraut
with piquant arugula cream
Soup

Serves 2: 1 small onion • 1 small potato • 1 tbs butter • 5 oz sauerkraut (drained) • 2 cups vegetable stock • 2 oz arugula • 1/4 cup crème fraîche • Salt to taste • Black pepper to taste

Peel and dice the onion and potato. Melt the butter in a saucepan over medium heat. Add the onion and potato and sauté until the onion is translucent. Add the sauerkraut and vegetable stock, cover, and simmer for 10 minutes. Wash and sort the arugula and puree it in a blender with the crème fraîche. Season with salt and pepper. Puree the soup, return it the saucepan, and bring it to the boiling point. Serve topped with the arugula cream.

PER PORTION: 211 calories • 3 g protein• 16 g fat • 16 g carbohydrates

Frothy Chervil
smooth and cleansing
Soup

Peel the onion and potatoes, and dice them coarsely. Melt the butter in a saucepan over medium heat. Add the onion and potatoes and sauté until the onion is translucent. Add the stock, cover, and simmer for at least 20 minutes over low heat.

Rinse the chervil, sort thoroughly, and shake dry. Set aside a little chervil for garnish. Chop the rest, and stir it into the soup.

Puree the soup and return it to the saucepan. Stir in the crème fraîche and heat the soup to the boiling point. Season with salt, pepper, and a little coriander. Whisk the soup with a hand blender or whisk to a frothy consistency, and garnish with the reserved chervil before serving.

Serves 2:
1 small onion
4 oz potatoes
1 tbs butter
2 cups chicken or vegetable stock
Large handful fresh chervil
1/4 cup crème fraîche
Salt to taste
White pepper to taste
Ground coriander to taste

Chervil
This delicate spring herb stimulates the circulation, cleanses the blood, and encourages the flow of urine and perspiration, all beneficial in a detox plan. It also has volatile oils and bitter constituents, which promote digestion by stimulating the secretion of stomach juices.

PER PORTION:
171 calories
6 g protein
15 g fat
14 g carbohydrates

Chervil in Aspic with
layers of appeal
Mustard Sauce

LIGHT DISHES & SNACKS

Boil the egg for 10 minutes, until the yolk is cooked hard. Rinse the egg in cold water and peel it. Wash, sort, and dry the chervil. Set aside a few pieces of chervil for garnish, wrapped in a clean, damp cloth and kept in a cool place. Chop the remaining chervil a little finer, and mix it into the stock.

Serves 2:
1 egg
Handful of fresh chervil
1/2 cup vegetable stock
1 pkg powdered gelatin
Salt to taste
White pepper to taste
Tabasco sauce to taste
2-3 tbs cottage cheese
3-4 tbs milk
1 tsp mild mustard

Sprinkle the gelatin over the stock in a saucepan and let stand for about 5 minutes. Heat gently, stirring, until the gelatin is fully dissolved.

Season the stock with salt, pepper, and Tabasco; the mixture should be piquant. Pour a small amount of the stock mixture into two ramekins or cups. Chill in the refrigerator until set.

Cut the egg in half crosswise. As soon as the gelatinized stock in the molds has set, place one half of the egg on each, cut-side down. Pour the remaining stock over the egg, and place in the refrigerator until set.

In a bowl, mix together the cottage cheese, milk, and mustard, and season with salt and pepper. Place the molds momentarily in hot water to loosen them, then invert them onto serving plates. Spoon a little sauce alongside each. Garnish with the reserved chervil and serve.

power

PER PORTION: 125 calories • 9 g protein • 5 g fat • 12 g carbohydrates

Light Herb
with radish vinaigrette
Mousse

Serves 2:

1 pkg powdered gelatin

1 bunch mixed fresh herbs, such as sorrel, flat-leaf parsley, dill, basil, and/or tarragon

5 tbs plain yogurt

Salt to taste

White pepper to taste

5 tbs heavy cream

5 radishes

2 tsp cider vinegar

2 tbs vegetable oil

Sprinkle the gelatin over a few tablespoons of water in a cup and let stand for 5 minutes. Warm the mixture by standing the cup in hot water; stir occasionally, until the gelatin has dissolved.

Wash and pick over the herbs, and shake dry. Set aside some of the herbs for garnish; chop the rest of the herbs finely.

Mix the dissolved gelatin with the yogurt and herbs. Season generously with salt and pepper.

Whip the cream until stiff, and fold it into the herb mixture. Transfer it to a small ring mold or to two cups. Cover, and place in the refrigerator to set.

Just before serving, wash, trim, and coarsely grate the radishes. Mix them with the cider vinegar and a little salt and pepper. Thoroughly beat in the oil with a whisk. Adjust the seasonings.

Place the mold or cups momentarily into hot water to loosen the edges. Invert the mousse onto a serving platter or plates. Garnish with herbs and pass the vinaigrette at the table.

PER PORTION: 215 calories • 4 g protein • 20 g fat • 3 g carbohydrates

Asparagus and Herb Omelet

succulent and quick to make

Serves 2: 9 oz green asparagus • Salt to taste • 2 tbs butter • 1 tsp sugar • 4 eggs • 2 tbs milk
• White pepper to taste • 2 tbs chopped fresh Italian parsley • 1-2 tbs chopped fresh chervil

Wash and trim the asparagus and steam it for 5-8 minutes over a little boiling salted water, with 1 tsp of the butter, and the sugar. In a bowl, whisk together the eggs, milk, salt, pepper, and herbs. Make two omelets one after the other in a nonstick skillet with the remaining butter. Drain the asparagus well, wrap in the omelets, and serve.

PER PORTION: 246 calories • 17 g protein • 17 g fat • 6 g carbohydrates

Brown Rice and Celery Root Pancakes

with herbed yogurt

Serves 2: 1/2 cup brown rice • Salt to taste • 5 tbs plain yogurt • 1 tbs cream cheese • White pepper to taste • 2 tbs chopped fresh herbs • 1 tsp unfiltered apple juice • 5 oz celery root • 2 eggs • Oil for frying

Cook the rice in 1 cup water until just tender, but still slightly firm, about 30 minutes. Mix the yogurt, cream cheese, salt, pepper, herbs, and apple juice. Peel and coarsely grate the celery root. Drain the rice, cool slightly, and mix with the celery root and eggs. Season with salt and pepper. Heat a small amount of oil in a skillet over medium-high heat. Spoon out portions of the rice mixture to fry a succession of small pancakes. Serve with the herbed yogurt.

PER PORTION: 354 calories • 13 g protein • 18 g fat • 36 g carbohydrates

Artichokes with a

imaginative company food

Duo of Dips

Place a large amount of salted water in a large saucepan with a few lemon slices. Cut off the stems of the artichokes. Cut off the top third of the leaves. Place the artichokes in the water and boil over medium heat for 40 minutes. The artichokes are cooked when the leaves can be pulled away easily. Boil the egg for 10 minutes, until the yolk is cooked hard. Peel and rinse the egg and separate the yolk and the white. Pass the yolk through a fine sieve, and mix it with the cider vinegar, salt, and pepper. Beat in the oil gradually. Wash the sorrel, shake dry, and remove the tough stalks. Chop the leaves. Dice the egg white finely. Mix the sorrel, egg white, and sour cream into the egg mixture. Season to taste; the mixture should be piquant. Wash, trim, and grate the radishes. Stir together the cream cheese and milk, season with salt, pepper, and a little cardamom; then stir in the grated radishes. Lift the artichokes out of the water and drain them. Serve with the dips.

Serves 2:
Salt to taste
Lemon slices
2 artichokes (about 18 oz each)
1 egg
2 tsp cider vinegar
White pepper to taste
3-4 tbs olive oil
1/2 bunch fresh sorrel
1/4 cup sour cream
1/2 bunch radishes
2 oz cream cheese
4-5 tbs milk
Ground cardamom to taste

Eating artichokes

Pull away one leaf at a time, holding the tops between your fingers. Dip the fleshy base of the leaf in one of the dips, and eat it by drawing the leaf base through your teeth to skim off the flesh of the vegetable. When you have pulled away all the leaves, you will find the inedible, fibrous "choke" in the middle. Scoop it out and underneath you will find the delicious, succulent "heart" of the artichoke.

PER PORTION:

381 calories

13 g protein

32 g fat

11 g carbohydrates

Cornmeal Patties
good eating at home or the office
with Radish Salad

Serves 2:

1/2 cup vegetable stock
1/3 cup cornmeal (finely ground)
1 small carrot
1 small kohlrabi
1/2 egg
1/2-1 bunch fresh dill
Salt to taste
Black pepper to taste
2-3 tbs bread crumbs
3 tbs vegetable oil
3/4 bunch radishes
2 tbs plain yogurt
1 tbs cream cheese
1/8 tsp ground cumin

Bring the vegetable stock to a boil. Add the cornmeal and cook over very low heat for 10 minutes, keeping the saucepan tightly covered. Peel the carrot and kohlrabi, and grate finely. Add the vegetables to the cornmeal and cook together for another 5 minutes. Transfer to a bowl. Stir in the egg and let the mixture cool a little.

Wash the dill and shake dry. Discard the tough stalks and chop. Stir the dill into the cornmeal mixture. Season with salt and pepper. Add enough bread crumbs to create a mixture that holds together well. Divide the mixture and shape into 4 equal-sized patties. Heat the oil in a nonstick skillet over medium-high heat. Fry the patties in the oil for 10 minutes over very low heat, turning occasionally.

Meanwhile, wash the radishes, and coarsely grate them. Stir together the grated radishes, yogurt, and cream cheese. Season with salt, pepper, and cumin. Serve to accompany the patties.

PER PORTION: 337 calories • 10 g protein • 18 g fat • 33 g carbohydrates

Ham and
with crunchy vegetables
Herb Dip

Cut the ham into very small dice. Wash, dry, and sort the herbs. Pluck the leaves away from the tough stalks. Reserve a few leaves for garnish, and chop the rest. Rinse the lemon in hot water and dry it. Grate the zest and squeeze the juice.

Mix the ham, herbs, lemon zest, lemon juice to taste, almonds, and cottage cheese. Season the dip generously with salt and pepper.

Remove the outer leaves of the endive. Cut the endive in half, and make a wedge-shaped cut to remove the core. Separate into individual leaves. Wash and trim the remaining vegetables. Cut them into long strips, just wide enough to manage easily when eating.

Arrange all the vegetables on a large platter, accompanied by the dip. Garnish with the reserved herbs and serve.

Serves 2:
2 oz boiled ham
Handful of fresh herbs
1/2 lemon
3 tbs chopped almonds
1/2 cup cottage cheese
Salt to taste
Black pepper to taste
1 head Belgian endive
1/2 small bunch celery
1 small zucchini
1 carrot
1 small kohlrabi
1 small red bell pepper

power

PER PORTION: 229 calories • 17 g protein • 12 g fat • 12 g carbohydrates

Asparagus and
chic and simple
Shrimp Risotto

Wash the asparagus, peel the lower third, and cut it into 1 1/4-1 1/2-inch pieces. Cut off the asparagus tips, cover, and set aside. Wash and trim the green onions. Cut the green parts diagonally into fine rings. Chop the white parts finely.

Heat the butter and oil in a skillet over medium heat. Add the white onion pieces and sauté until translucent. Add the pieces of asparagus stem, followed by the rice. Sauté briefly and pour in the wine. Cook over low heat, stirring occasionally, until the rice has absorbed all the liquid. Add the vegetable stock about 1/3 cup at a time, and cook, stirring occasionally, allowing each addition to be absorbed before adding the next.

Serves 2:
9 oz asparagus
1/2 bunch green onions
1 tbs butter
2 tsp olive oil
7 oz Arborio rice
1/2 cup dry white wine
2 cups vegetable stock
Salt to taste
White pepper to taste
4 oz peeled cooked shrimp
1 oz Parmesan cheese, freshly grated

After 10 minutes, stir in the asparagus tips and the green pieces of green onion. Cook the rice until tender, but still slightly firm in the center; the mixture should remain creamy. Add the shrimp, mix, and heat through. Season the risotto with salt and pepper, and sprinkle with Parmesan before serving.

PER PORTION: 622 calories • 26 g protein • 12 g fat • 85 g carbohydrates

Stuffed
with mushroom and ham filling
Artichokes

Preheat the oven to 350°F. Bring a large amount of salted water to a boil in a large saucepan, and add the lemon juice or vinegar. Cut off the stems of the artichokes. Remove the outer

Serves 2:
Salt to taste
2 tbs lemon juice or vinegar
2 large globe artichokes
1 onion
5 oz small white mushrooms
1 clove garlic
2 tbs olive oil
2 oz boiled ham
1-2 sprigs each fresh thyme, rosemary, parsley, and basil
2 slices whole-grain bread
2 oz Swiss cheese, grated
Black pepper to taste

leaves, and trim off the tops of any very pointed leaves. Boil the artichokes in the water for 40 minutes over medium heat. They are cooked when the leaves can be pulled away easily and the bottom of the artichoke feels soft when a small knife is inserted into it.

Peel the onion and chop finely. Clean, trim, and chop the mushrooms. Peel and finely mince the garlic. Heat the oil in a skillet over medium heat. Add the onion and sauté until translucent. Add the garlic and mushrooms, and sauté over low heat for 5 minutes. Dice the ham finely. Wash, dry, and chop the herbs. Stir the ham and herbs into the mushroom mixture, and remove from the heat.

Lift the artichokes out of the water, and drain them thoroughly upside down. Fold open the outer leaves and pull out the soft leaves from the middle. Remove the hairy, inedible "choke" with a spoon, and discard.

Cut the bread into small dice, add to the mushroom mixture, and stir in the cheese. Season with salt and pepper. Stuff the artichokes with the filling. Place the stuffed artichokes side by side in an ovenproof dish, and bake in the middle of the oven for 20 minutes, until hot.

PER PORTION: 366 calories • 22 g protein • 21 g fat • 21 g carbohydrates

Salmon with

delicious served with new potatoes

Sorrel Sauce

Wash and sort the sorrel. Set aside a few leaves and chop the rest. Peel and finely chop the shallot. Melt 1/2 tbs of the butter in a small saucepan over medium heat. Add the shallot and sauté until translucent. Sprinkle with the flour, and cook briefly, stirring. Stir in the stock. Add the chopped sorrel. Cover, and simmer over low heat for 5 minutes.

Rinse the salmon fillets in cold water and pat dry. Melt the remaining 1/2 tbs butter in a nonstick skillet until frothy. Cook the salmon over low heat for 3-5 minutes on each side.

Stir the crème fraîche into the sorrel sauce and season with salt, pepper, and a pinch of sugar. Cut the remaining sorrel leaves into fine strips. Arrange the salmon and sauce on plates, and scatter strips of sorrel on top before serving.

Serves 2:

2 oz fresh sorrel

1 shallot

1 tbs butter

1/2 tbs flour

1 cup salmon stock or other fish stock

2 salmon fillets (6 oz each)

2-3 tbs crème fraîche

Salt to taste

White pepper to taste

Sugar

Sorrel

This lemony herb is rich in iron, vitamin C, and bitter constituents. It stimulates the appetite, has a diuretic effect, and promotes blood formation and cleansing. It is also beneficial to the liver. However, sorrel should not be eaten in excessive quantities, because the oxalic acid it contains forms insoluble calcium salts, which can lead to kidney stones.

PER PORTION:

438 calories

36 g protein

35 g fat

5 g carbohydrates

power

Multicolored

Asian inspiration with hot spices and vitamins

Vegetable Curry

Slit open the chiles and remove the seeds. Wash and chop the chiles. Peel and chop the garlic and ginger. In a saucepan, heat the coconut cream with the stock, soy sauce, and curry paste until heated through.

Serves 2:
1-2 red chiles
1 clove garlic
1/2 oz fresh ginger
1/4 cup coconut cream (unsweetened)
6 tbs vegetable stock
2 tbs soy sauce
1 tbs curry paste
2 stalks celery
1 carrot
1/2 bunch green onions
3 oz broccoli
2 oz bean sprouts
2 tbs vegetable oil
2 sprigs fresh mint

Wash and trim and/or peel the celery, carrot, green onions, and broccoli. Slice the celery, carrot, and green onions finely. Separate the broccoli into small florets. Rinse the bean sprouts and drain thoroughly.

Heat the oil in a wok or skillet over medium-high heat. Add the chile and stir-fry for 1 minute. Add the celery, carrot, green onions, and broccoli, and stir-fry for another 2-3 minutes. Add the bean sprouts and stir-fry for another 3 minutes.

Pour the coconut sauce into the wok, and cook all the ingredients together for 1-2 minutes. Just before serving, wash and dry the mint and cut the leaves into thin strips. Sprinkle the mint over the vegetables and serve immediately.

power

PER PORTION: 245 calories • 20 g protein • 20 g fat • 12 g carbohydrates

Simmered
with broccoli and sheep's milk cheese
Red Lentils

Serves 2: 9 oz broccoli • 1 small onion • 1 tbs olive oil • 1/2 cup red lentils • 1 cup vegetable stock • Salt to taste • Black pepper to taste • 1 tsp fresh thyme leaves • 4 oz sheep's milk cheese

Wash and trim the broccoli and separate it into florets. Peel the onion, dice it finely, and sauté it in the oil in a wide skillet until translucent. Add the broccoli, lentils, stock, salt, pepper, and thyme. Cook for 15 minutes, until the lentils are tender. Crumble the cheese, and add to the lentils. Cook together for another minute, until heated through.

Per Portion: 364 calories • 25 g protein • 14 g fat • 33 g carbohydrates

Vegetable and
a meatless meal from the oven
Yogurt Bake

Serves 2: • 1 1/4 lb mixed vegetables • 3 eggs • 8 oz whole-milk yogurt • 1 tsp flour • 1 oz chopped almonds • Salt to taste • Black pepper to taste • 1/2 bunch fresh Italian parsley • 1/2 bunch peppercress

Preheat the oven to 400°F. Wash and trim the vegetables, and cut into bite-sized pieces. Boil them for 5 minutes in a small amount of water; drain well. Separate the egg yolks from the whites. Mix the yogurt, flour, chopped almonds, salt, pepper, chopped parsley, cress, and egg yolks. Beat the egg whites until stiff and fold them into the mixture. Place the vegetables in a baking dish and pour the yogurt mixture over the top. Bake in the middle of the oven for 20-25 minutes, until set.

Per Portion: 380 calories • 22 g protein • 21 g fat • 24 g carbohydrates

Asparagus Gratin with

with Swiss cheese and almonds

Herb Cream

Preheat the oven to 400°F. Wash and trim the asparagus and peel the lower third of the stalks. Bring a small amount of water to a boil in a saucepan with the salt, sugar, and butter. Place the asparagus in a steamer insert and lower into the saucepan. Cook, covered, for 5-8 minutes, until tender-crisp.

Butter a shallow ovenproof dish. Wash the herbs and shake dry. Strip the leaves from the herb stalks and chop them finely. In a bowl, mix the herbs, sour cream, and eggs. Season with salt and pepper.

Drain the asparagus thoroughly and place it in the buttered baking dish. Pour the herb-cream mixture over the top. Sprinkle with the cheese and almonds, and bake in the middle of the oven for 30 minutes.

Serves 2:

1 lb asparagus

Salt to taste

Sugar to taste

1 tsp butter

2 sprigs fresh tarragon

2 sprigs fresh thyme

2 sprigs fresh lemon balm or sorrel

1 cup sour cream

2 eggs

White pepper to taste

2 oz Swiss cheese, grated

2 tbs sliced almonds

PER PORTION: 483 calories • 20 g protein • 41 g fat • 9 g carbohydrates

Linguine with
stylish and cleansing
Artichoke Sauce

Place a large amount of water in a saucepan, and add the lemon juice or vinegar and a little salt. Cut off the stems of the artichokes. Cut off the top half of the leaves. Pull off or trim the remaining leaves, and peel around the hearts with a sharp knife. Scrape out the inedible, hairy "choke" with a spoon. Immediately place the trimmed artichoke hearts into the pan of water. Bring to a boil, then cook for about 10 minutes, until the hearts are tender. Lift out and drain the artichoke hearts, then cut into pieces.

Peel and chop the onion. Peel the garlic and cut into strips. Wash the herbs, shake dry, and roughly chop the leaves. In another saucepan, bring a generous amount of salted water to a boil (use at least 2 quarts). Add the pasta and cook until just tender, but still slightly firm to the bite (*al dente*).

In a medium skillet, heat the oil over medium-low heat. Add the onion and garlic and sauté until translucent. Add the artichoke hearts and herbs. Add the wine, season with salt and pepper, and simmer gently until heated through.

Drain the pasta well and add it to the other ingredients in the skillet; mix well. Sprinkle with the Parmesan before serving.

Serves 2:

2 tbs fresh lemon juice or wine vinegar

Salt to taste

2 large artichokes

1 medium red onion

2 small cloves garlic

2 sprigs each fresh thyme and marjoram

1 small sprig fresh rosemary

8 oz linguine or spaghetti

6 tbs olive oil

6 tbs rosé wine

Black pepper to taste

2 oz Parmesan cheese, freshly grated

power

PER PORTION: 763 calories • 27 g protein • 31 g fat • 88 g carbohydrates

Quick Potato

a spicy Indian-style cleanser

Curry

Wash and peel the potatoes and cut into bite-sized chunks. Heat the oil in a large skillet. Fry the potatoes over medium heat for about 20 minutes,

Serves 2:
14 oz boiling potatoes
1 tbs vegetable oil
2 small tomatoes
1/2 bunch green onions
1 clove garlic
1/2 oz fresh ginger
1/2-1 green chile
1/2 tsp garam masala
1/4 tsp flour
4 oz plain whole-milk yogurt
1 tbs fresh lemon juice
Salt to taste
Black pepper to taste
1-2 tsp black sesame seeds

stirring and turning frequently, until tender. Cut an X in the round ends of the tomatoes. Plunge them into boiling water for a few moments, then remove the peels with a pairing knife. Cut the tomato flesh into dice. Wash and trim the green onions. Slice them finely into rings, reserving a little of the green portions for garnish. Peel the garlic and ginger. Slit open, trim, and wash the chile. Chop the garlic, ginger, and chile, and add to the skillet with the potatoes, together with the green onions. Sauté the mixture briefly and stir in the garam masala. In a bowl, blend the flour and yogurt until smooth. Stir into the potato mixture, then add the tomatoes. Cook over low heat for another 10 minutes.

Season the potato mixture with the lemon juice, salt, and pepper. Sprinkle with the green onion pieces and sesame seeds, and serve immediately.

PER PORTION: 205 calories • 6 g protein • 7 g fat • 30 g carbohydrates

Asparagus and Chicken Stir-Fry

a fresh Asian-style combination

Serves 2: 1/2 bunch green onions • 2 oz shiitake mushrooms • 1 carrot • 14 oz asparagus • 7 oz boneless chicken breast • 1 tbs canola oil • 1 tbs soy sauce • 5 tbs dry white wine • Black pepper to taste

Wash, trim, and chop the onions, mushrooms, and carrot. Wash the asparagus, peel the lower third of the stalks, and cut into pieces. Cut the chicken into cubes. Heat the oil in a wok over medium-high heat, and stir-fry the asparagus and carrot for 3 minutes. Add the mushrooms and onions, and stir-fry for 2 minutes. Move the vegetables aside and stir-fry the chicken until browned on all sides. Add the soy sauce and wine, season, and stir-fry all ingredients for 3 minutes.

PER PORTION: 309 calories • 32 g protein • 6 g fat • 31 g carbohydrates

Tagliatelle with Asparagus

a quick and delicious dish

Serves 2: 1 onion • 9 oz asparagus • Salt to taste • 7 oz spinach tagliatelle • 1 tbs butter • 1/2 cup vegetable stock • 4 oz cream cheese • White pepper to taste• Fresh chervil leaves

Peel and finely dice the onion. Wash, trim, and peel the asparagus. Slice it, leaving the tips whole. Cook the pasta in boiling salted water until just tender and drain. Meanwhile, sauté the onion and asparagus in the butter until the onion is translucent. Add the stock, cream cheese, salt, and pepper. Cover and cook for 10 minutes. Garnish with chervil and serve with the pasta.

PER PORTION: 551 calories • 18 g protein • 20 g fat • 77 g carbohydrates

Asparagus and
with stylish red rice
Chicken Ragout

Serves 2:

1 lb white or green asparagus

3 cups water

Salt to taste

1/4 tsp sugar

2/3 cup red rice or brown rice

7 oz boneless chicken breast

White pepper to taste

2 tbs butter

1 tbs flour

1 cup chicken stock

2 sprigs fresh chervil or Italian parsley

Wash and trim and asparagus and peel the lower third of the stalks. In a saucepan, bring 1 cup of the water to a boil with some salt and the sugar. Place the asparagus in a steamer insert and lower it into the pan. Cover with a tight-fitting lid and steam for 5-8 minutes, until the asparagus is tender-crisp. Drain, reserving the cooking liquid. Cut the asparagus into 1 1/4-inch pieces.

Meanwhile, bring the remaining 2 cups water to a boil in a saucepan. Add the rice, cover the pan tightly, and cook over low heat for 30-40 minutes, until the rice has absorbed all of the water. Meanwhile, rinse the chicken in cold water and pat dry. Cut it into 1-inch cubes and season with pepper.

Melt the butter in a saucepan over medium-high heat. Add the chicken and cook until golden brown on all sides; remove from the pan. Sprinkle the flour into the butter, stir, and cook until golden. Stir in the stock, blending it in well.

Pour in the asparagus cooking liquid, and cook over high heat, stirring, until the mixture becomes creamy. Wash the chervil or parsley, and chop or tear it into pieces. Stir it into the sauce, and add the asparagus and chicken. Return to a boil, season with salt and pepper, and serve with the rice.

PER PORTION: 494 calories • 34 g protein • 14 g fat • 65 g carbohydrates

Index

Abbreviations
tsp = teaspoon
tbs = tablespoon

Published originally under the title
ENTSCHLACKEN MIT GENUSS: Für
Vitalität und Wohlbefinden

©1999 Gräfe und Unzer Verlag GmbH,
Munich
English translation copyright for the US
edition: © 2000 Silverback Books, Inc.

Editors: Ina Schröter, Jennifer Newens, CCP
Readers: Dipl. oec. troph. Maryna Zimdars,
Vené Franco
Layout and design: Heinz Kraxenberger
Production: Helmut Giersberg,
Shanti Nelson
Photos: FoodPhotography Eising, Munich
Typeset: Easy Pic Library, Munich
Reproduction: Repro Schmidt, Dornbirn
Printing: Appl, Wemding
Binding: Sellier, Freising

ISBN: 1-930603-25-8

Caution

The techniques and recipes in this book are
to be used at the reader's sole discretion
and risk. Always consult a doctor before
beginning a new eating plan.

Angelika Ilies

A native of Hamburg, Germany, Angelika
Ilies studied ecotrophology, and launched
her career immediately on completion of her
studies. She gained experience of the
everyday realities of publishing with a
renowned publishing house in London.
Returning to her home country, she
employed her skills in the service of
Germany's biggest food magazine. Since
1989, she has enjoyed a successful career as a
freelance author and food journalist.

Susie M. and **Pete Eising** have studios in
Munich, Germany, and Kennebunkport,
Maine, U.S.A. They studied at the
Fachakademie für Fotodesign in Munich,
where they established their own food
photography studio in 1991.

For this book:
Photographic design:
Martina Gorlach
Food Stylist:
Monika Schuster

SILVERBACK

BOOKS, INC.

www.silverbackbooks.com